BY DIXIE J. WHITTED

DAHLER & NICHOLLS FIGHT CRIME! (CRIME WINS)

WHAT COULD GO WRONG?

CRIME RHYMES: FROM BAD TO VERSE

CRIME RHYMES:
FROM BAD TO VERSE

DIXIE J. WHITTED

Best Wishes —
Dixie J. Whitted

Elphinstone Press

Copyright © 2017 Dixie J Whitted

All rights reserved. No part of this publication may be reproduced, distributed, or transmitted in any form or by any means, including photocopying, recording, or other electronic or mechanical methods, without the prior written permission of the publisher, except in the case of brief quotations embodied in critical reviews and certain other noncommercial uses permitted by copyright law.

For permission requests, write to the publisher, addressed "Attention: Permissions Coordinator," at the website below.

Several of these verses have been previously published in *Ellery Queen's Mystery Magazine* and in *The Armchair Detective*.
(Thanks, fellas.)

Elphinstone Press
www.dixiejwhitted.com

Printed in the United States of America

FIRST EDITION
10 9 8 7 6 5 4 3 2 1

PAPERBACK ISBN-13: 978-1-5464-1614-2
PAPERBACK ISBN-10: 1-5464-1614-5

Also Available in eBook Format

DEDICATION

To:
My Beloved Mother,
Who Taught Me
To Read
And Write
And Draw.

CONTENTS

LETHAL LITTLE LIMERICKS, ETC. 9

HOLMES, SWEET HOLMES 71

LIZZIE BORDEN* TOOK AN AXE** 93

SPECIAL BONUS FEATURE:
THE ADVENTURE OF
THE STAINLESS SPINSTER 107

LETHAL LITTLE LIMERICKS, ETC.

PROMOTION NOTION

A consulting detective named Keate
Didn't earn enough money to eat.
Now he's rolling in dough
For a few weeks ago
He wrote "MEN" on the door of his suite.

TO THE PAROLE BOARD:

Headstrong housewife Henrietta
Fed her husband strychnine stew.
Now she says she's coping better—
Can she come and live with you?

OVERKILLED

The inspector asked, "What have you got?"
Sighed the coroner, "Rather a lot.
An unpopular beast
Was the recent deceased:
He's been stabbed, poisoned, strangled and shot!"

"I'LL NEVER BE HUNGRY AGAIN …"

Scarlett's kidnappers wrote, "Come and get 'er!"
And they added, "The sooner, the better!"
Rhett might have complied
And recovered his bride,
But Rhett's setter had eaten the letter …

DIMINISHED CAPACITY

"We're all agreed," the foreman said,
"We've talked it through and through.
The defendant's innocent, you see,
By reason of insanity ..."
Judge: "What?—All twelve of you?!"

SMOOTH OPERATOR

Sam sanded down his fingertips—
He knew a burglar sometimes slips ...
In custody now, Sam can smile:
His fingerprints are on the file.

IVA ARCHER'S REVENGE

The sergeant finally solved the crime
With the private eye's invaluable aid
(When the private eye could spare the time
From seducing every available maid ...)
The sobbing murderess had confessed
And now that the final scene was played,
The sarge said to Effie, half in jest,
"You really ought to get Sam spayed ..."

SELF-EMPLOYED

Growled Big Al, who was facing the chair,
"I'll walk out of here free as air.
Though I've slain thirty-three,
They've got nothin' on me!"
The I.R.S. said "Au contraire …"

INFAMOUS LAST WORDS

To his murderous nephew, Frank sent,
"I'm sure of your crime you'll repent:
For now that I'm buried,
Your plan has miscarried;
I spent every cent 'ere I went!"

FANGS FOR THE MEMORIES

Cat burglar Archibald Scugg
Tried to purloin a rare Persian rug,
But he found his hands full
With the owner's pit bull …
Now he's snug as a bug—in the jug.

PURR-FECT CRIME

O'Neal reassured Miss MacFee,
"Your jewels don't interest me."
As he stuffed her Maltese
Into his valise,
He said, "I'm a cat burglar, you see."

WURST CASE SCENARIO

Adolph Luetgert, Sausage King,
Slew his wife for money
But overlooked her wedding ring ...
Does your hot dog taste funny?

OPEN WIDE ...

An unbalanced dentist, McTavity,
Was found out in his latest depravity:
When he buried his spouse
In the wood near their house,
He neglected to fill in the cavity.

THIS PIECE GOES HERE

Pretty Flossie lost her head
When she met a handsome stranger.
"Be careful, dear," her best friends said,
But Flossie scoffed at danger.
Her head's still missing, says Sergeant Krupp,
But other bits keep turning up.

SPADE WORK NEEDED

"There's a client out here you ought to see:
He's tracing his father, aged ninety-three."
The Eye looked up, a scowl on his face.
"Not *another* doddering-wanderer case!"

FOR ART'S SAKE

Artie painted like Renoir,
El Greco, Turner, and Degas.
He had a secret clientele
Who paid him quietly and well.
He "borrowed" Van Gogh's "Starry Night";
He knew no one would spot the fake …
His copy turned out swell, all right—
He sold the real one by mistake.

24-HOUR SERVICE

Phil was holding up a convenience store;
He had just emptied out the till,
When an off-duty cop came in just to shop—
Which was quite inconvenient for Phil.

NURTURING NATURE

Politically-correct Mr. Hyde
Is on the environment's side:
He recycles all waste
And has somehow misplaced
His biodegradable bride ...

FORGING AHEAD

Pete's penmanship was unexciting,
A fault that practice often cures;
He makes his living now by writing
Other people's signatures.

ALL WET

Mr. Flynn found his romance impeded.
A mishap was what his scheme needed.
If the husband were drowned,
It would work, but he found
That his victim swam better than he did.

"AS TOLD TO"

A grasping ghost-writer, Miss Vale,
Used to blackmail her clients by mail.
She dwelt on each sin
Until one turned her in;
Now she's writing her memoirs in jail.

FAMILY PLOT

Old Frank had lived well, beyond doubt,
Though he never threw money about.
But his masquerade slipped
When they opened the crypt
And his long-lost twin brother fell out.

CANDID VIDEO

Wally was the wheelman
(He just got out of jail);
Eddie planned the route for their escape.
The bank job went like clockwork,
Except for one detail:
The passerby who got it all on tape.

YOU CAN'T GET GOOD HELP NO MORE

A slack-jawed mechanic named Ross
Does odd jobs for a Mafia boss.
Told to rig the ignition
Of his chief's competition,
He blew up his own car. No loss.

COTTAGE INDUSTRY

A boarding-house keeper, Miss Bard,
Found that renting her rooms wasn't hard.
She collected each pension
With careful attention
Till the officers dug up her yard ...

BLUNT REMEDY

Arsenics, antimonies, cyanides, curares
Are aids used by impatient beneficiaries.
But they leave a trail digestive
And few druggists keep a stock:
Frank's nephew, growing restive,
Hit him with a rock.

MY LITTLE FRICASSEE

A heavy-set lady named Fryer
Was the wife of a cooking-ware buyer.
To shed his plump spouse,
He burned down the house
And giggled, "The fat's in the fire ..."

PROGRESS?

I think we can take it as read:
Modern crime's just a bash on the head.
Though genteel and subtle
(How those butlers could buttle!)
The country-house murder is dead.

HIS FAREWELL APPEARANCE

An actor, grown tired of his wife,
Had just made his point—with a knife—
When the door opened wide,
Cameramen streamed inside,
And Ralph Edwards said, "*This*—is Your *Life!*"

WHOLLY ELEMENTARY

The detective said modestly, "Rot!"
When they dug up the late Mr. Scott.
"You all might have inferred
Where the corpse was interred:
There's an obvious hole in this plot!"

"PLEASE OMIT FLOWERS"

Mary had an allergy
That bordered on psychosis;
Her husband, wishing to be free,
Just murdered her—with roses.

CRIME RHYMES: FROM BAD TO VERSE

NEVER TEASE THE COOK

Pretty Penelope Plowder
Is ladylike if you don't crowd her.
Her fiancé Jack
Dropped a clam down her back—
Don't ask what she put in the chowder.

OVER THE WALL

An escape artist known as "The Eel"
Used his specialized talents to steal.
It stopped being fun
When he pulled Murder One—
He wants jumping beans for his last meal.

ANOTHER FINE MESS

Sneered Susan to Stan, "You've grown lardy—
You're fatter than Oliver Hardy!"
Chagrined by their quarrels,
He dug 'neath the laurels
And buried her in the back yard-y.

ALL IN THE DAY'S WORK

An unlucky locksmith named Moore
Was picked up in a raid—was he sore!
Asked why he was there,
He was quick to declare,
"I was making a bolt for the door!"

DOUBLE YOUR MONEY

On his copier, Reginald dotes,
And the excellent work it promotes.
The colors are true
And the details sharp too:
He runs off perfect century notes.

FIENDS IN HIGH PLACES

The reporter fulfilled his ambition:
Got the goods on a bent politician.
He splashed the guy's capers
All over the papers,
But that was his Final Edition ...

WHEELER-DEALER

As a jewel thief, Moss worked alone,
Perfecting techniques all his own.
As he drove past a femme
With a ten-carat gem,
Though rolling, Moss gathered the stone.

MAN'S BEST FRIEND?

"My wife's left and I'm on my own,"
Moaned lonely grass-widower Sloan.
He was bearing up well,
So the neighbors did tell,
Until Fido dug up the wrong bone.

JURIS-IMPRUDENCE

A criminal lawyer named Sharpe
At the jury would bellow and carp.
He annoyed them one day
In his usual way—
Now his client is playing a harp.

PROFESSIONAL COURTESY

A pawnbroker known as "The Leech"
Gave vent to a horrible screech
When the tide pulled him down
And he thought he would drown—
But a shark spat him back on the beach.

SPARKLING CYANIDE

Mr. Blandford, a wine connoisseur,
Murmured, "This was an excellent year ..."
Then he slumped in his place
With a smile on his face;
His widow remarked, "Try the *bier.*"

NEATNESS COUNTS

A languid young lass named Estelle
Was a maid in an uptown hotel.
In each room she cleaned,
Several keepsakes she gleaned;
Now she's sweeping the floor of her cell.

A NATURAL MISTAKE

The beautiful Lady Sylvester
Had a husband who thought he would test her.
But his near-sighted mate
Shot him down—it was late—
She thought he'd broken in to molest her.

ALL THAT GLITTERS

"Salty" Smith dealt in gold-mining stock.
His investors were in for a shock:
Drilling got under way,
But on opening day
They took out fifty tons of pure rock.

WILL THAT BE ALL, SIR?

The butler has hidden the knife
With which Lord Renault slew his wife.
People frequently say
That crime doesn't pay,
But the butler is now fixed for life.

SKILLED LABORER

In an ivy-clad cottage at Wopping
Lives notorious axe-slayer Topping.
Paroled now for good,
He purveys firewood,
Satisfying his penchant for chopping ...

POETIC JUSTICE

A writer of humorous verse
To his friends was considered a curse.
His penultimate pun
Was an ode-ious one,
So his last vehicle was a hearse.

THE TELL-TALE TONGUE

A gossipy witch was Miss Quack;
Her tongue stabbed her friends in the back.
Now her body's been found
And the suspects abound—
Of mourners, there's somehow a lack.

LAST BEQUEST

An embalmer with very few clients
On his wealthy wife's death placed reliance.
But, divining his plot,
She said, as she shot,
"I've donated *your* organs to science!"

LEGAL EAGLE

The law is Malone's great obsession;
He's unbeatable at his profession.
His spellbinding style
Just climaxed a trial
With the district attorney's confession!

FIRED WITH ENTHUSIASM

Failed businessman Billingsworth Blore
Bought disaster insurance galore;
He planned to retire
Right after the fire,
But his henchman burned down the wrong store.

KEYHOLE POSITION

Miss Fitch doesn't chafe in her fetters
Though her stipend depends on her betters.
In her governess trade
She is handsomely paid—
By her blackmailing poison-pen letters.

THE TIE THAT BINDS

Chester got the better grades,
Had his way with buxom maids,
Made the teams for which I tried,
Over-achieving far and wide.
Today I said, "Well, that's the lot!"
When Chester grabbed my parking spot.
And, your Honor, that is why
I strangled him with our old school tie.

A LITTLE BIRD TOLD THEM

Wife-slayer Archibald Smoot
Sobbed, "This must be the work of a brute ..."
Abashed by his grieving,
The cops were just leaving
When the parakeet screeched, "Arch—don't shoot!"

PLEA-SING BARGAIN

Bernie ratted on his friends.
(He's not their Valentine.)
In one short year, his sentence ends—
A snitch in time saved nine.

DE-RAILED

Big Bert had a very small brain:
He decided to hold up a train.
His plan of attack
Was to stand on the track ...
The express will be late once again.

FAIRY TALE

The defendant shivered in the dock,
On trial for his crime.
"Let's have your story," snapped Judge Brock.
"Well, once upon a time ..."

SIMPLY NOT DONE

In England, which won't arm a cop,
The courts ruled that hangings must stop.
Still, those crooks steeped in vice
Should make one think twice—
They were bad to the very last drop.

BREAKING NEW GROUND

While leaving the plane he had skyjacked,
D. B. Cooper prepared for his last act:
As he jumped out with glee,
He thought he was home free—
But his parachute opened on impact ...

HANKY-PANKY

Hank had a good job in a bank;
He had his rich uncle to thank.
But youth can be rash
And one day the bank's cash
Went along to Hawaii with Hank.

JUSTIFIABLE HOMICIDE

A widow named Mrs. McClory
Has just sent her husband to glory.
He read faster than she did;
Though she whimpered and pleaded,
He would tell her the *end* of the story.

CHUTZPAH UNLIMITED

Wicked Walter slew his parents
To obtain his legacy.
On the grounds that he was orphaned,
He requested clemency.
The judge, on being sent for,
Soon denied him a parole:
"You're the perfect argument for
Retroactive birth control!"

MAIDEN'S CURSE

After shedding the fourth Mrs. Keller
(Whose friends had attempted to tell her),
He curled his moustache
To impress his new pash—
There's plenty of room in the cellar.

FOREGONE CONCLUSION

Barrister Harrington Brew
Pled "insanity" till he was blue;
As usual, it worked—
His client then smirked,
"I'm not crazy enough to pay *you!*"

HE WANTS TO BE ALONE

The boss has a contract on Jerry
'Cause he sang like a big fat canary.
He breaks each prison rule;
He's nobody's fool:
He feels safe when he's in solitary.

MOVING VIOLATION

She's taking her lawyer's advice:
Her black frock is simple and nice.
She ran into her spouse
On the hill near their house,
And somehow backed over him twice ...

TRIGGER MORTIS

Wild Bill liked to brag of his past
And to boast of his draw lightning-fast.
He insulted a gent
In a bar argument,
And his first draw in years was his last.

ALL CHOKED UP

Stan plotted a fake suicide—
His insurance would go to his bride.
He would join her in Spain
With their ill-gotten gain—
But the noose was too expertly tied.

VERTIGO? NOT VERY

Orlando, the mad Duke of Claris,
Had lured his rich bride to the terrace.
He murmured sedately,
"I've killed no one lately ...
Lean out for the best view of Paris ..."

DRUMMING UP TRADE

A serial killer named Powers
Gave the cops some uncomfortable hours.
When tracked to his store,
He said business was poor:
He supplied wreaths and funeral flowers.

CHEAP MATERIÉL

Terrorist Fellingwell Frost
Showed new recruits how to cut cost:
"Now try to keep calm
While I wire this bomb—"
The rest of the sentence was lost.

CASE DISSOLVED

Walt knew why his late wife had picked him:
Her nagging tongue needed a victim.
A barrel of acid
Soon rendered her placid—
But her dentures survived to convict him.

CALORIES DO COUNT

The chocolates sent to Miss Keats
Were arsenic-laden sweetmeats.
The lesson is ample:
My dears, never sample
Anonymous edible treats.

LAST STRAW

A fastidious landlord named Baxter
Whose tenant claimed housecleaning taxed her,
Overlooked the clogged drains
And opaque window panes,
But when she planted grass, Baxter axed her.

ON THE OTHER HAND …

Do-gooder Fenimore Foley
Thought prison reforms moved too slowly.
He promoted a bill
Preaching kindness, until
He was mugged by a recent parolee.

TAKEN FROM LIFE

A sculptor of ladies sans clothes
Can't part with them after they pose.
That group in the hall,
The "Three Graces" and all—
The one in the middle is Rose.

THE PHILOSOPHER

Sir Cedric mused, "Battle and strife
Take so much of the joy out of life."
With a world-weary sigh,
He adjusted his tie—
In a knot 'round the neck of his wife.

HANDYMAN SPECIAL

Detailed to trace Mrs. Loring,
The officers found their task boring.
Their laxness was fateful,
But her husband was grateful
That they didn't look under the flooring ...

SILENCE IS GOLDEN

Harridan Hepzibah Horner
Was meeting her mate on the corner.
He started to call
When he saw the safe fall,
But didn't dare speak up and warn her.

SNAKE ATTACK

Molly and Zeke run a pet boutique;
Their profits fluctuate, week to week.
They just caught a burglar, wrigglin' and writhin'—
Instead of a watch dog, they use a python.

THE HAND IS QUICKER

The corpse on the library floor
Of the room locked the evening before
Was stabbed by Lord Lyme,
Who accomplished his crime
By being the first through the door.

END OF THE LINE

'Round the death bed of feeble Lord Loverd
Like vultures his greedy heirs hovered.
"I've cut you all off
With a shilling (cough, cough)!"
They died of the shock—*he* recovered.

HE WAS RIGHT

A miserly bachelor named Bhaer
Feared his death was desired by his heir.
Although old, he was spry,
But he failed to espy
The string at the top of the stair ...

STUCK TO HIS LAST

Backing out of the bank with a glare,
Duke growled, "Everyone hold it right there!"
As he raced for the street
Wet cement clutched his feet:
The sidewalk was up for repair.

PRACTICE MAKES PROFIT

A computer programmer named Phil
Was a hacker of no little skill.
With a confident smile,
He broke into a file
And altered his rich uncle's will.

THE CURE-ALL

Nervous Nancy Applebaum
Abuses drugs to "keep her calm."
They put her in a pleasant haze—
She hasn't moved for three whole days.

CLOSE CONFINEMENT

A crook with a price on his head
Hid under Aunt Agatha's bed.
She found him down there
Like an answer to prayer;
Now he's longing for prison instead.

PRE-MORTEM

The coroner sharpened his knife
And sighed as he honed it, "That's life.
We just never know
When it's our time to go ..."
And called, "Come in, dear—" to his wife.

FOR OLD CRIME'S SAKE

"Let's pull one last job," wheezed old Perce.
But senility can be a curse:
When Elmer and Frank
Tottered out of the bank,
Old Perce put the car in reverse ...

ONE COLD WINTER NIGHT

The Earl took a pull on his briar
And added a log to the fire.
He bent a rapt gaze
On the comforting blaze—
Which composed his wife's funeral pyre ...

BAD TIDINGS

The shifty-eyed bridegroom denied
He'd disposed of his elderly bride.
He was living quite well
At their seaside hotel
Until she came in with the tide ...

OOPS ...

Gat Grice was a hood on a roll,
Making off with the payroll he stole,
But he ran out of luck
When his gas pedal stuck—
He rear-ended the Highway Patrol.

GUILT BY ASSOCIATION

A Siamese twin slew his mother
And was tried, with his innocent brother.
The judge looked bemused
As he viewed the accused:
"*Must* you be so attached to each other?"

COLD COMFORT

The village of Rasping-on-Bone
Is a poor place to visit alone:
Its sinister inn
Serves a poisonous gin,
And the hospital's not on the phone.

OUT-FLANKED

Here, outlined in chalk, is feckless Frank,
Gunned down while robbing his fourteenth bank.
As a frequent felon, he was in the first rank,
But at dodging bullets, frankly, Frank stank.

IF AT FIRST …

Miss Bidewell has broken her fast
And captured a husband at last.
It's a beautiful match
But there's one little catch:
There are five missing brides in his past.

QUICK ACQUITTAL

A felon named Fauntleroy Fittle
Said he'd had a sad childhood when little.
The tale of his fears
Had the courtroom in tears—
The jury returned, non-committal.

BOOMERANG

The hit man that Mrs. Hobbs hired
To dispose of her husband, retired,
Said the price was a joke
And shrugged as he spoke,
"He offered me double—" and fired.

SWEET AND DEADLY

Aunt Fannie is known for her fondant,
With butter and sugar abundant.
Her late husband, Mitch,
Ate a lot … It's so rich
That the ant paste was really redundant.

FALSE SECURITY

Alone in her flat, Mrs. Byrd
Shrugged off the odd noises she heard.
"At seventy-three,
Who would bother with me?"
Headline: "Lunatic Slayer Claims Third."

FOUR-LEGGED FRAUD

A gold-bricking watchdog named Rover
Is currently living in clover:
 He gets steak every day
 (And has hidden away
The leash that the burglar tripped over.)

PERFECT CRIME?

Joe's wife is a shrew and a half;
She took sleeping pills for a laugh.
Said the doc, "They won't take
If you keep her awake …"
Joe brewed a large pot of de-caff.

BLOOD WILL TELL

The killer went over the place;
Of his crime, he destroyed every trace.
The last "i" was dotted—
Till officers spotted
The fingernail marks on his face …

AN OLD FLAME

An addle-brained widow named Fern,
Who was known to have money to burn,
Encountered a cad
Through a lonely-hearts ad—
That's Fern over there in the urn.

PASSION'S PLAYTHING

The owner of Bertha's Boutique
Read four romance novels each week,
So she fell easy prey
To a handsome *roué*—
Nobody heard her last shriek.

THE BETTER TO EAT YOU

Red Ridinghood got a surprise
When she gazed into Wolfie's big eyes.
But the woodcutter's zeal
Turned him into a meal—
Now she's selling "Wolfburgers and Fries."

TILL CASH DO US PART

Stan said they'd retire once they scored;
His bride acquiesced, as if bored.
But the beautiful Brenda
Had a hidden agenda:
She fingered him for the reward.

KEEPING IT SIMPLE

Corrigan, walking his beat,
Tripped over a corpse in the street.
It was on Caravelle,
Which is tricky to spell—
So he lugged the stiff over to Treat.

INTERIOR DECORATION

Ray wanted a rug for his floor.
At the zoo, he had heard tigers roar.
He sneaked in after dark
For a hide, for a lark ...
The service is Friday, at four.

SOLID ASSETS

A former bank robber named Marden
Had buried his loot in the garden,
But his wife, hating clover,
Cemented it over.
Now he's watching his larcenies harden ...

A LIKELY YARN

Mrs. Horatia Green
Was slain by her knitting machine.
She was cabled and purled
Swiftly out of this world.
(Her husband had just left the scene.)

OCCUPATIONAL HAZARD

Safecracker Barnaby Budge
Is now just a puddle of sludge.
While trimming the fuse
He was planning to use,
His pal gave the nitro a nudge ...

SOUND EFFECTS

A clever mechanic named Reese
Said, "These auto break-ins must cease!"
He's installed a device
That makes vandals think twice:
His car alarm screams, "Help, Police!"

OUR MAN IN THE STREET

News anchor Bellamy Breen
Never passed up a chance to be seen;
He confronted the gun
Of a crook on the run ...
His body is lower left screen.

TELL-TALE TERRAIN

Greg strangled his girlfriend Marie
And buried her under a tree,
But after the rain,
He was asked to explain
The sunken spot, six feet by three ...

SNOW JOB

A hit man sent out from Chicago
Caught up with his quarry in Fargo;
He had just shot his man
When the blizzard began—
And he found he could not make his car go ...

TRADE SECRET

Grinned Lawyer Malone, "I don't worry
About honest citizens' fury.
For a large enough fee,
I set murderers free—
By selecting a nice, stupid jury."

HE SEEMED SO SINCERE

They caught Jim bent over the form
Of his seventeenth victim, still warm.
He was out on parole
For the good of his soul—
After giving his *word* he'd reform.

LESS THAN KIN

Black crepe decorated the doors
At the home of the Harrowby-Moores.
"Well, John," sighed Celeste,
"Your mother's at rest ..."
"*My* mother?—I thought she was *yours!*"

DEATH INSURANCE

Pauline's married life was a joke:
She was usually barefoot and broke.
But she turned the tables;
She's now wearing sables—
She encouraged her husband to smoke ...

WHILE THE IRON IS HOT

Suzanne sliced the mushrooms with skill
For the steak she would serve Uncle Bill.
Then she seasoned the brew
With a toadstool or two
To prevent him from changing his will.

DIXIE J. WHITTED

FANGS A LOT

Veterinarian Hjalimar Hake,
Whose nagging wife kept him awake,
For better or worse
Slipped into her purse
Patricia, his pet coral snake ...

FISHY TALE

Poor relative Phillipa Fairing
Took her rich aunt for an airing.
The wheelchair's weak brake
Gave way near the lake;
Now Aunt's a reluctant red herring ...

SUCH A DEAL

A gangland mortician named Meek
Had a two-for-one special last week:
For a limited time
He would compound a crime
With a false-bottomed coffin, non-leak.

UNHAPPY ENDING

Bank teller Pettigrew Vance
Loved to read about crime and romance.
When faced by a crook,
He "went by the book";
Now they're picking lead out of his pants.

WINDOW DRESSING

Something moans nights at Harrowby Hall
And there's blood on the scullery wall …
Explained the sly hosts,
"Before we had 'ghosts,'
We never could rent it at all."

FORCED OUTSOURCING

A gang lord both strict and penurious
Warned his mob that the cops might get curious.
As they poured the concrete
All over his feet,
They blandly said, "That doesn't worry us."

SOUP'S OFF

Milt hated the cook his wife hired:
"Fat homely old broads should be fired!"
He sneered upon Florence
With lordly abhorrence,
Tasted the soup—and expired …

OVER-EAGER

Said old Frank to his nephew, Ralph Rowes,
"You know you're my heir, I suppose?"
Ralph fawned, "What can I do
To show my thanks to you?"
"Take your foot off my oxygen hose!"

ROAD HOG

Sheriff Schwein roamed the whole countryside;
He had speed traps set up far and wide.
He was really in clover
Until he pulled over
Bank robbers Bonnie and Clyde …

APT PUPIL

At burglary, Mallory shone:
He made others' baubles his own,
Till a girl stole his heart,
Not to mention his art …
And his watch and his car and his phone.

COSMETIC MEDIC

Doc Carver's the crooks' favorite quack:
When displayed on the post office rack,
They can get a new chin
Or a Hollywood grin.
"Satisfaction—or your old face back!"

SHOOTING PAINS

An escaping bank robber named Bannon
Was passing a circus and ran in.
He dressed as a clown
Till the heat should die down—
Now he's being shot out of a cannon.

WEIGHTY ISSUE

Arrested, Bernard muttered, "Zounds!"
(He was too fat to outrun the hounds.)
As the guillotine descended,
The crowd comprehended
That he'd lost ten superfluous pounds ...

REVENGE IS SWEET?

The chocolates came by the post,
A gift from a guest to a host.
Lord Lofford ate two,
Turned an odd shade of blue,
And quietly gave up the ghost.

SORRY HE ASKED

The séance took place after three.
They'd managed to reach Aunt Marie.
"Are you happy?" asked Fred.
"I wouldn't be *dead*
If *you* hadn't poisoned my tea!"

HOLMES, SWEET HOLMES

OR

"Though he might be more humble, there's no police like Holmes." — E. W. Hornung (creator of Raffles and brother-in-law of Sir Arthur Conan Doyle)

AN UN-SEAMLY POSITION

Holmes had cornered a prominent Red;
As he hung from a beam overhead,
He felt himself slipping—
His trousers were ripping.
"Quick, Watson—a needle—and thread!"

HOLMES ON THE CASE

Oh, give me a Holmes
Where the mastermind roams
And the ponce and the pickpocket prey.
For discouraging sin
Is where Sherlock comes in,
And the fog never lifts, night or day.

Holmes, Holmes, never change ...
With Watson, your colleague and friend ...
The game is afoot
And you're in hot pursuit—
Moriarty will lose in the end.

ONE MUST DRAW THE LINE

Holmes pitted his wits and resources
Against wicked arch-criminal forces.
His standards were high—
Royalty might apply.
Of course, *he* never handled divorces.

HIS LAST CURTSY?

When Holmes, dressed in female attire,
Trod the boards to unmask the fiend Myer,
His role on the stage
Became London's new rage;
Now his fan club won't let him retire.

FIRST THINGS FIRST

Doctor Watson helped Holmes to detect;
Their triumphs continued unchecked.
He felt quite a glow
As they vanquished each foe.
True, his *patients* succumbed to neglect ...

DEBT BLOW

After tracing a killer from Kent,
With his money and energy spent,
Holmes found on his door
The dread Sign of Four:
"Butcher, Baker, Suit-maker and Rent."

PERHAPS SCARLET FOR THE STUDY?

Holmes' rooms were infested with mice,
So he took Doctor Watson's advice
And acquired a ferret
To lodge in the garret—
He's had to repaint the place twice ...

A MELANCHOLY AIR

What is that lugubrious sound?
Some weird Baskervillian Hound?
People shudder and moan
At its uncanny groan—
It's only Holmes, fiddling around.

NOBLESSE OBLIGES

Holmes remarked to Edwardius Rex,
"Your Majesty's brilliance reflects
Your swiftness of thought.
Here's the letter you sought.
Remember, no personal cheques."

THE FALSE PANACEA

A smile wreathed the good doctor's face.
"I have saved my friend Holmes from disgrace!
His morphine addiction
Will soon be a fiction:
Cure-all *heroin's* taking its place."

ASK THE EXPERT

Lestrade chewed his moustache in pique.
"We've had eight unsolved murders this week…"
Holmes ironically bowed
And sighed, "Why be proud?—
You know you had only to speak."

AN OUNCE OF PREVENTION

Holmes tendered the coachman a shilling
And said, "Kindly wait here, if you're willing.
For the Ripper's about—
If you see him, please shout.
I shall then put an end to his killing."

A STUDY IN CONTRASTS

"It was Lady Godiva, of course,
Who put all she had on a horse,"
Watson happily snickered.
Holmes' gaze merely flickered
As he frostily said, "Don't be coarse!"

X MARKS THE SPOT

On holiday, roaming the stalls,
Coloured postcards for sale on the walls,
Watson purchased a few
For his friends, old and new.
Holmes' read: "Yours till Reichenbach Falls."

CELESTIAL SLEUTH

As Sherlock reclined on a cloud,
God asked, "Could you pick Eve from this crowd?"
"Elementary, Sir,"
Holmes said, with a purr.
"*She* has *no navel.*" He bowed.

NO PROPHET HE

Doctor Watson, by Holmes long befriended
(Though not for an intellect splendid),
As he toyed with a kipper,
Pronounced, "Jack the Ripper
Will speedily be apprehended."

BIPOLAR CHOLER?

Moriarty's uncouth oscillation
Was the source of his foul fascination:
His snake-like aspect
Caused Holmes to reflect,
"This fiend needs a nice long vacation."

EVERYONE'S A CRITIC

Holmes smiled as he took up his bow,
"This selection will please you, I know."
From a neighboring flat
Came the shout, "Kill that cat!"
A well-aimed workman's boot laid Holmes low.

BACK IN HARNESS

Yawned Watson, "We've been in a rut."
Holmes answered him mildly, "Tut, tut.
I've perfected a plan
To catch Colonel Moran ...
The game is afoot—let's kick butt!"

THE PERFECT HOUSEKEEPER

Mrs. Hudson deserves our huzzahs
For long-suffering *je ne sais quois;*
Holmes' habits nocturnal
(We cite Watson's journal)
Must often have given her pause.

SHE WAS NOT AMUSED

Moriarty leapt into a hansom
And crept up to Her Majesty's transom.
He would kidnap the queen
In his flying machine,
And demand Holmes' retirement as ransom.

...OF SUMATRAN ORIGIN

When called to a financier's flat
To track down a fairly large rat,
"You're wasting my time,"
Holmes sniffed. "I fight crime—
I suggest, sir, you purchase a cat!"

MASTER OF DISGUISE

Importuned by a ragged old stew,
Watson helped him along with his shoe.
As he sprawled in the gutter
And started to sputter,
Watson said, "Sorry, Holmes—if that's *you* ..."

GOOD RIDDANCE

The duchess sobbed into her port
And implored Holmes to lend his support:
"Whatever the cost,
Help my husband *stay* lost—
He's quite short, with a hideous wart!"

ROYALTY FLUSHED

Holmes studied the rug through his glass.
"I detect indications of grass
Of the type only seen
On the Queen's putting green ..."
Lestrade grimly muttered, "I pass!"

... AND STEELY FINGERS

Holmes lighted his pipe with a coal
Whose heat singed the rim of the bowl.
Gasped Watson, "What nerve!—
Why, your hand didn't swerve!"
"It requires an iron self-control."

ACHTUNG SCHWEINHUND!

Lestrade said, "Herr Soames, don't be rash.
We've uncovered your weaponry cache."
"I am ruined!" shrieked Soames.
"Natürlich," smiled Holmes,
Ripping off his false Kaiser moustache.

A HAIRY TALE

As the Giant Rat sprang for his throat,
Holmes fended it off with his coat.
"Shoot, Watson!—" snapped he,
"—Or else this will be
The shortest adventure you wrote!"

FOOD FOR THOUGHT

Holmes gazed at his meal with disdain.
"Such stuff cannot nourish the brain."
As he toyed with his salad
His features grew pallid.
"Mrs. Hudson is *slimming* again!"

IT'S ALWAYS SOMETHING

Watson asked Holmes, "Why so glum?
The Baskerville's Hound has grown dumb.
The vile 'Speckled Band'
You scotched out of hand,
And wrapped up the 'Engineer's Thumb.'"

PROBLEM SERVANT

In Aberdeen, seeking a clue,
Holmes noticed mud smeared on his shoe.
"Good heavens!" he muttered.
"The toast wasn't *buttered* …
The *false butler* slew the whole crew!"

REPTILIAN VILLAIN

Doctor Watson was caught by surprise
Gazing into a cobra's red eyes ...
With a smile of good cheer,
Holmes remarked, "Never fear!"
And slipped into his mongoose disguise.

EXCUSE ME?

After solving the death of Lord Linnet,
Holmes discussed the complexities in it.
"Surely, it's plain
To the most feeble brain—
Oh, Watson, come here for a minute ..."

THE GAME'S A FEAT

In spite of the arch-villain's ruses,
Holmes never had need of excuses.
As the last card was placed,
Moriarty grimaced.
Said Holmes, "I deduced you held deuces."

SHORT TRIP

As the duchess leaped into her boat,
Holmes fingered the bruise on his throat.
"She'll escape!" Watson cried.
Holmes shrugged and replied,
"She won't get very far in the moat."

STOP THE MUSIC!

Moriarty, arch-villain nefarious,
Rigged a bomb inside Holmes' Stradivarius.
On noting its weight,
Holmes became quite irate.
"That fiend seems determined to bury us!"

LONDON PARTICULAR

While choking on fog at the dockside,
Watson at Holmes goggled ox-eyed.
Gasped Holmes, "Here's the trail;
Try not to inhale—
At least it's not carbon monoxide."

DRAT THE LUCK!

Holmes narrowly missed Moriarty
As the latter was leaving a party.
(The party was dead
From a blow on the head.)
Holmes' curses were varied and hearty.

IT'S A KNACK

Holmes questioned each suspect in turn
While Lestrade did his usual slow burn.
"I fail to surmise
How you sort truth from lies."
Smiled Holmes, "If you listen, you'll learn."

NO CASE TOO SMALL

Music-hall queen Lylah Lee
Hired Holmes to recover her flea.
"He's a stage-trained *artiste*,
That droll little beast—"
Holmes suddenly scratched. "Is this he?"

HE OBSERVED KEENLY

Said Holmes to his barber, "I fear
You've imbibed too much whisky or beer.
My deduction arose
From the hue of your nose ...
By the way, would you hand me my ear?"

THE NOSE KNOWS

Holmes' eyes had the gleam of a snake;
He rapped, "Watson, make no mistake!
We must plan this campaign
For our ultimate gain—
Mrs. Hudson is baking a cake!"

JUDGMENT VINDICATED

Holmes tasted the dregs of the sherry,
Then spat, as it seemed necessary.
He regarded the form
Of Lord Wormwood, still warm:
"How wise I was never to marry!"

HE NEARLY SMILED

Moriarty, escaping a pinch,
Left his trousers behind on a winch.
Informed of the joke,
Holmes' self-control broke:
His lip twitched an eighth of an inch.

VICE DE-FEETED

As the footpad careened down the cobbles,
"Stop, Thief!" bellowed Constable Pobbles.
With a smartly-aimed kick
Holmes disabled Black Dick.
You may see him at Dartmoor—he hobbles.

HE SENT IT BACK

While humming a charming etude,
Holmes languidly picked at his food
And said, "Moriarty,
I'm enjoying your party.
Is this arsenic?—Don't think me rude."

ONCE MORE INTO THE BREACH

Holmes, by old age overtaken,
Yet proved his detractors mistaken:
Although geriatric
He pulled a last hat trick
And rescued the Empire's bacon.

HOW SWEET IT IS

Then Holmes said to Watson, "Old chum,
The time for retirement's come.
I shall temper my ease
With the keeping of bees.
You may title this tale, 'Hum, Sweet Hum.'"

CRIME RHYMES: FROM BAD TO VERSE

LIZZIE BORDEN* TOOK AN AXE** ...

AND GAVE HER MOTHER*** FORTY**** WHACKS.

WHEN SHE SAW WHAT SHE HAD DONE,
SHE GAVE HER FATHER FORTY-ONE***** ...

*Or An Unknown Assailant.
**A Hatchet.
***Stepmother.
****Nineteen.
*****Eleven.

AUGUST 3, 1892

Said Abbie to Andrew, "My dear,
Lizzie's been acting—well, queer.
The store bread looked nice
So I asked for a slice.
The cleaver passed right by my ear!"

BREAKFAST AT THE BORDENS'

Lizzie lifted the lid of the pot
Of mutton broth, greasy and hot;
She wrinkled her nose
As her nausea rose—
Her thoughts turned to crime on the spot.

STRONG MOTIVATION

Lizzie longed for a loftier station,
With sirloin—not mutton—for ration.
Stoutly determined
To be sabled and ermined,
Her solution caused quite a sensation ...

PASTORAL PROLOGUE

Such August heat!—Hell could not match it.
The screen door sags loose on its latchet ...
While down in the cellar
A grim Cinderella,
Miss Lizzie sits, honing a hatchet.

AX HER NO QUESTIONS

Abbie's chores in the guest room were licit:
Cleaning up after Uncle John's visit.
But she wasn't alone—
Came her stepdaughter's tone:
"Mrs. Borden..." "Well, Lizzie, what *is* it?"

AX-IDENTAL DEATH

Folding his hands in his lap,
Mr. Borden stretched out for a nap.
His stupor was deep,
But he moaned in his sleep
At the sound of the Grim Reaper's rap ...

OR A CUP OF PRUSSIC ACID?

Miss Lizzie put on her new cloak
(The neighbors were fashionable folk).
Thus gently attired
She politely inquired,
"Could I borrow your hatchet?—Ours broke."

PREMONITION

Dr. Bowen did all he could do,
But old Borden would never come to.
He rose to his feet.
"Do you have a clean sheet?"
Lizzie spoke up then: "Better get two ..."

NEATNESS COUNTS

A heat wave was gripping the town
When some fiend cut the old Bordens down,
But the jury grew dizzy
Confronted by Lizzie
And her sweet little bloodless blue gown.

UP HER SLEEVE?

For trial Lizzie Borden was bound
And the newspapermen gathered 'round.
They were certain she did it;
The hatchet?—she hid it—
So well that it's never been found.

YANKEE INGENUITY

The funeral morn dawned bright and clear,
A boon for one entrepreneur.
With a nod to Miss Lizzie,
He promptly got busy:
"Get your souvenir hatchets right here!"

THE CUT DIRECT

Consider bucolic Fall River,
Whose matrons indignantly quiver.
Miss Borden's renown
Brings tourists to town—
They profit, but cannot forgive her.

REFERENCE: LIZZIE BORDEN

Bridget Sullivan said, "Death and taxes
Is sure, but I'll tell you the facts is:
Windows I'll do,
Scrub the scullery, too,
But I *won't* work no place where there's *axes!*"

PROPHYL-AX-IS

"This heat drags me down," Borden said.
"I think I'll stretch out on my bed."
But Lizzie'd a plan:
"Rest on the divan.
I'll get something for your poor head ..."

OUT, DAMNED SPOT

In the days when a horse drew the hearse
Red hair was considered a curse.
As Lizzie well knew,
When her parents she slew,
Red *hands* were considered much worse ...

THAT'S FIT TO PRINT?

Reporters named Graham and Gordon
Evaded the officers' cordon:
"As the sorrowing daughter
At this scene of slaughter,
May we have a statement, Miss Borden?"

SISTERS IN MISFORTUNE

Said Lizzie to Emma, "This dress
Is covered with paint—it's a mess.
And since I can't turn it,
I may as well burn it ..."
Said Emma, "I couldn't care less."

CLIENT CONFIDENCE

The Borden trial opened its session;
Lawyer Jennings adorned his profession.
When Lizzie went free
Through his advocacy,
He shuddered—and burned her confession ...

FOR THE DEFENSE

Miss Emma spoke up for her sister:
"... So gentle, a child could resist her ..."
Lizzie watched her defender
("... Her hands are so tender ...")
And pensively picked at a blister.

SHARP RETORT

The Borden case seems like a hoax,
With poor Lizzie the butt of bad jokes:
"We're having a fair.
Do you think you'll be there?"
"Just a minute—I'll go axe my folks ..."

ALWAYS THE LADY

Miss Lizzie declined to be heard,
So her advocates had the last word;
They based her defense
On their chauvinist sense
That her "feminine weakness" had stirred.

POSTSCRIPT: FALL RIVER

You think Lizzie's guilty?—She ain't.
Her parents just came over faint.
Not even a glutton
Survives rancid mutton:
They both died of "summer complaint."

HAUNTED HISTORY

The Borden tale hasn't an ending
Though its sorrows are long past amending.
The house in Fall River
Makes passersby shiver
At the sounds of a hatchet, descending ...

CODA
OR
OH, SHUT UP, LIZZIE

The Borden plot has turf to hide them
From the pitying eyes that espied them.
Though they've signed a long lease,
They can't rest in peace
With Lizzie there, giggling beside them ...

THE LAST WORD

Against Lizzie, there was no case:
No blood on her hands, clothes or face.
And after the crime
There just wasn't time
For her to erase every trace.

SPECIAL BONUS FEATURE

THE ADVENTURE OF
THE STAINLESS SPINSTER

In the summer of 1893, prim 33-year-old New England spinster Lizzie Borden stood before the bar of justice accused of an infamous crime: the brutal hatchet murders of her aged father and stepmother. Echoes of the case still reverberate down the years and opinions on the verdict, then as now, remain sharply divided.

Among those who have interested themselves in this classic Murder-of-the-Century are the world's first consulting detective and his loyal friend and associate, Sherlock Holmes and Dr. John Watson.

* * *

"I call it monstrous, Holmes—monstrous! What can that jury have been thinking?"

Such were my pardonably heated remarks as I entered the familiar Baker Street environs that morning to find Sherlock Holmes seated at the table before the fireplace with the accoutrements of breakfast before him. I cast down the newspaper that had aroused my wrath upon the leather settee near the fireplace and divested myself of my greatcoat as I spoke.

Holmes glanced up from his plate and reproved me mildly.

"Pray compose yourself, Watson. Try some of Mrs. Hudson's admirable braised kidneys, do. And set your mind at rest: the verdict was perfectly unimpeachable."

I sat down rather heavily, shaking my head.

"Holmes, are we speaking of the same case? You can't possibly be referring—"

"To the notorious Borden murders of Fall River, Massachusetts, in America? Of course."

"Then I am indeed at a loss to comprehend your statement. Miss Borden was obviously the murderess and should certainly have been convicted."

Holmes pushed aside his plate, stood and reached a long arm for his pipe on the mantelpiece. He picked up the Persian slipper in which he keeps the peculiarly aromatic shag tobacco that has done so much to discolour Mrs. Hudson's walls and draperies and inserted a generous amount in the bowl of his pipe. Using the fireplace tongs, he possessed himself of a glowing coal and applied it to the tobacco; when it was well alight he puffed at it thoughtfully and began pacing up and down the room.

"As you are aware, I have been studying this affair since its inception, and have also arranged to receive newspaper accounts from the American cutting bureaus dealing with the events as they transpired. From a careful study of the facts—admixed with not a little fiction, as is usual with the customary rush of ink-stained wretches to get their stories published ahead of their competitors regardless of accuracy—I have reached my own conclusions."

"And you believe Lizzie Borden to be innocent? But, Holmes, the *evidence!*"

Holmes laughed sardonically.

"'Evidence'? In the words of that admirable former journalist and author, Bret Harte, 'I wouldn't hang a yellow dog on such "evidence"...'"

He sat down at the long mahogany table near the window and drew forth a leather-bound tome from a row of similar volumes containing records of criminal investigations that had attracted his professional interest. Opening it, he rapidly perused several pages and then indicated a certain paragraph with a satisfied nod.

"As you doubtless recall, the infamous double murder took place on August 4th, 1892, in that narrow two-story house on Second Street in Fall River. It was a stifling hot day and there were ripe and rotting pears lying under the aged pear tree in the back garden near the barn ..."

I nodded and replied, "The barn where Lizzie *said* she

had spent perhaps twenty minutes upstairs in seeking out some lead weights for fishing sinkers, whilst eating pears. But the police officers who later searched the barn found no trace of her footprints."

"Watson, Watson. At the trial, it was brought out that two young boys had also been inside the barn that morning—and on the second floor—before the officers arrived. They testified on the witness stand to that effect."

"Even so—"

"And an itinerant ice-cream peddler who had been passing the residence at the crucial time stated on oath that he had seen Miss Lizzie leave the barn and make her way toward the house."

I shrugged.

Holmes resumed, "At the time of the murders, only four persons were known to be in the house: Mr. and Mrs. Borden, Lizzie, and the maid, Bridget Sullivan. I believe that a fifth person entered unobserved and remained on the premises long enough to encompass both crimes."

"Do you refer to Miss Emma, Lizzie's elder sister? But surely she was proved to have been visiting friends at some distance away."

"Not she. There is no possibility of her having absented herself for several hours from her hosts, yet returning in time to receive the telegram breaking the news of the deaths."

I was still at sea; I couldn't imagine what Holmes was driving at. I picked up a fork and speared one of Mrs. Hudson's kidneys which had grown rather cold but was still quite savory.

"It was, of course, *Mr.* Borden who was the intended victim," Holmes went on. "Mrs. Borden was an accidental obstacle that had to be removed."

I poured myself a cup of tea and added two lumps of sugar, then took up the last crumpet and spread it with a copious amount of Messrs. Crosse & Blackwell's excellent orange marmalade. I felt the need of fortification in the face of Holmes' amazing insinuations. Why, all the world knew that Lizzie Borden had nourished an implacable aversion toward her stepmother. Surely, she alone could have wielded that hatchet with such murderous zeal!

Not for the first time Holmes appeared to divine my thoughts.

"My dear chap, 'what the soldier said isn't evidence' as you are well aware. If in every household in which there are persons who are scarcely on speaking terms such a situation inevitably led to bloody murder, the population would be decimated overnight.

"No, the key to these crimes lies in the character of Andrew Borden. He was, by all accounts, a singularly miserly and ill-tempered individual who had incurred the enmity of a great many persons during his seventy years."

"Then it is your contention that a disgruntled business associate lay in wait to assassinate him?"

"Not precisely. There was someone much nearer home, as we may say, to whom he had given recent—and doubtless, prior—provocation."

Although I confess to a certain skepticism, if Holmes

was indeed on the scent of some hitherto unsuspected miscreant I was willing to hear him out. I adjusted my expression to one of hopeful expectation.

Holmes continued, "Let us consider the events leading up to that morning. The family had all been suffering digestive discomforts for two days, probably as a result of the spoiled viands of which they had been partaking: tainted swordfish, rancid mutton, and the villainous johnny-cakes which I believe to be composed of some coarse ground meal combined with fat and fried ... So ill were they that Abby Borden had hurried across the street on the day before the murders in order to seek the advice of their neighbor, Dr. Bowen. When she brought him into her husband's presence, Borden flew into a rage at the prospect of a fee for this visit and, snarling, 'My money shan't pay for it!' ordered the doctor out of the house.

"Later, Lizzie remarked to her friend Miss Russell, 'I was so ashamed at the way Father treated Dr. Bowen; I was so mortified.'

"A trivial incident, perhaps. But the Bowens had lived across the street from the Borden family for twenty years... There may well have been a festering unpleasantness between the two men.

"To pass on to the crimes: Mrs. Borden was found in the guest bedroom upstairs. She had been murdered, it was conjectured, during the ninety-minute period whilst her husband was making his daily downtown business rounds. He himself was killed within a few minutes of his return home.

"It is important to note that neither Mrs. Borden nor Lizzie should have been expected to be at home that morning. Lizzie had made plans to go to a summer cottage with some friends, and Mrs. Borden had received a note requesting her to visit some person who was ailing—"

I broke in. "Lizzie said there was such a note, but no one ever came forward to confirm it."

"Patience, Watson, patience. The murderer expected to enter an empty house saving only the presence of the maid, whose custom it was to lie down for a rest in her attic room after completing her morning chores. He would await Borden's return from his usual downtown errands—of which he was well aware, having observed them over a period of time—accomplish his purpose and leave unobserved. But circumstances dictated otherwise."

Holmes turned back to the leather-bound book and beckoned me to his side. With his lean index finger he traced a newspaper diagram depicting the lower and upper floor plans of 92 Second Street, the Borden home.

"When he entered the house via this side door, which had been left unlocked all morning while the maid washed the windows, he made his way through the kitchen and parlour and from thence mounted the front stairs and concealed himself in the large closet at the head of the staircase. Shortly thereafter, hearing footsteps in the guest bedroom next door he presumed that Andrew Borden had returned home. Quietly entering the room, hatchet in hand—he was unexpectedly confronted by *Mrs.* Borden..."

"Good God, Holmes!"

"Indeed. Our killer's plans had to be altered in an instant; here before him stood a witness who could not be allowed to give an alarm. He struck, and struck again in a fever of manic urgency ... and then he nerved himself to retrieve a certain piece of incriminating evidence from Abby's apron pocket. Shaken, I have no doubt, he once more concealed himself in the closet and set himself to wait for his intended victim."

"I still can't see who this straw man might be, Holmes—some former employee with a grudge, or was it perhaps Uncle John Morse to whom you refer?"

Holmes looked an interrogation at me.

"John Vinnicum Morse, Borden's brother-in-law by his first marriage?" he inquired, smiling.

I sat back comfortably, pluming myself on having for once penetrated Holmes' meaning before he could elucidate his arcane reasoning processes.

Holmes sighed and shot me a pitying glance.

"You surely must remember the results of the police investigation. Mr. Morse had arrived the day before, spent the night at the Borden residence—which is why Mrs. Borden was engaged in making up the guest room bed when she was surprised and slain—and early on the morning of the crimes he had left the house and did not return until some time after the bodies were discovered. His alibi was tested in every respect and was vouched for by several witnesses.

"No, I postulate our slayer to have been an 'invisible' professional man, above suspicion, who dresses in formal black no matter what the weather, who carries a commodious satchel as a matter of business, who is familiar with his neighbors' comings and goings and can plan accordingly."

"Not—"

"Yes. Dr. Bowen. Whose dark suit would readily absorb any bloodstains that bypassed his waterproof surgical apron and whose use of that recent medical innovation of rubber gloves would prevent such unseemly traces as those on the hands of Lady Macbeth.

"You cited the famous note that was never seen again. Later, as police detectives were investigating the murder scene, Dr. Bowen was observed to dispose of a note in the kitchen stove. Asked about it, he replied that it was 'something about my daughter, going someplace.' No one bothered to examine that piece of paper. And who more likely than the doctor to have given it to Mrs. Borden, with written directions for her to call upon someone who was ill?"

"And that was the evidence in her pocket?"

"A very likely surmise."

I ruminated.

"But, Holmes, why a hatchet as a murder instrument? Surely it is the last weapon one would expect a doctor to use."

"Excellent, Watson! You have answered your own question.

"After disposing of Andrew Borden, he then left the house immediately—which probably saved Lizzie's life. When she returned from the barn, the screen door was still ajar ... and she had not left it in that position. Had she entered the house moments earlier, can you doubt that there would have been a third corpse on the premises?"

Holmes continued, "And, not to digress, but cast your mind back over the curious circumstance of the state of Miss Lizzie's clothing on that dreadful day."

"I don't understand you, Holmes. As I recall, there were no bloodstains to be seen on Miss Lizzie's clothing or person."

"Precisely—that was the curious circumstance. That, and the fact that the murder weapon has never been discovered."

"But, the broken hatchet the police officers found in the cellar—"

"Was sent to Harvard University for examination and their forensic laboratory was unable to discern any trace of blood upon it. Furthermore, the blade was old and blunt whereas the murder weapon was keen and sharp."

I must have looked dubious for Holmes leaned forward and tapped my knee with his forefinger.

"Look here, Watson. In your privileged position as a married man, let me inquire of you: how long does it take your wife to attire herself for the street?"

I flushed at the question.

"Really, Holmes—"

"My dear fellow, I am merely seeking information."

I reflected.

"Well, I suppose between twenty to thirty minutes

would be an average length of time. After all, there are various under-linens, hosiery, and all those confounded buttons and loops. I don't suppose that Mary owns a dress with fewer than two dozen buttons—down the back, up the sleeves ..."

"As I surmised. And Lizzie Borden, if guilty, would have first needed to remove any stained clothing and then re-clothe herself in an immaculate frock. No woman could have done it in the time."

"To return to the events of that day, when Lizzie came indoors from the barn and discovered her father's body her first action was to call the maid, Bridget, down from her room. Lizzie asked her to run across the street and fetch the doctor. Bridget returned in minutes, along with neighbors Mrs. Churchill and Alice Russell who rallied to Lizzie's side, but no doctor. The doctor's wife had given her to understand that he was 'out on his rounds.'

"Yet Dr. Bowen *did* arrive a very few moments later. When he examined Borden's body, as he later testified, 'blood was still flowing from his [Borden's] wounds' and he appeared to have expired 'within the last twenty minutes.' Ample time for the murderer to clear away any tell-tale traces on his person, but not time for Lizzie—who had entered scant moments before—to wash her hands, change her clothing and successfully conceal any bloodstained garments as well as the instrument of death!"

I leaned back in my chair and smiled.

"Aren't you forgetting about the dress that Lizzie burned?" I asked demurely.

"Not at all. That dress had previously been soiled with paint as Miss Emma, Miss Alice Russell and the dressmaker each testified. It was hanging on a nail near the kitchen in plain view during the time that three separate police searches were made; it is incredible to imagine that any clothing that must have been fouled with a great effusion of blood could have gone unnoticed. And remember: Lizzie burned the dress in full view and with the knowledge and approbation of her sister and Miss Russell—in broad daylight with several police officers still on the premises."

"Stop a moment, Holmes. Was there not a theory that the murderer had stood behind the parlour door while wielding the hatchet that killed Andrew Borden? And that the door would have protected the assailant from bloodstains?"

"My dear Watson ..." The lean finger tapped the diagram once again. "As you can clearly see, that door opens *outwardly* from the parlour. An orangutan might have managed to lurk in that recess and still extend an arm far enough to strike those sanguinary blows, but no ordinary human being could have done so."

I was not yet defeated.

"I find it very difficult to believe that the doctor or anyone else from outside the household could have remained concealed on the premises for the length of time required. Was it not established that some ninety minutes had elapsed between the first and second murders?"

"Established? Or opined? And who was our authority for the timing of the killings?" Holmes leaned forward, transfixing me with his sharp grey eyes.

"The good doctor, who was so providentially prompt on the scene, gave it as his opinion that Mrs. Borden had predeceased her husband by perhaps an hour to an hour and a half. The police medical examiner arrived later that afternoon and concurred with his colleague's findings, but did not perform the autopsies until the following day. Considering that the slayings took place during a period of scorching August heat, blood would coagulate very rapidly which could well contribute to a conveniently erroneous conclusion."

I capitulated.

"And the murder weapon—I suppose it would have fitted neatly into the doctor's bag?"

"Indubitably. Along with a rolled-up apron, gloves and cotton or lint bandages to absorb stains ..."

I surrendered, stood up and offered him my hand.

"I apologize for my hard thoughts about the jurymen's intelligence and I offer a belated *mea culpa* for *my* erroneous conclusions regarding Miss Borden. And now Holmes, are you going to set your deductions before the proper American authorities so that justice may be done?"

Holmes arose, tapped the dottle of burnt ash in his pipe bowl out upon the hearthstone and regarded me with a smile.

"I think ... not, Watson. Miss Borden has been acquitted, I have not been requested to intervene in the case and naturally do not wish to intrude my theories upon an unresponsive audience."

"But, Holmes ..."

"And besides, my esteemed brother Mycroft has himself made a close study of the evidence and has reached an entirely different conclusion! Unless I can persuade him that my solution is the correct one, I am honour-bound to defer to his unequalled acumen."

I was dumbfounded.

"A different conclusion? How is that possible? Your deductions seem to me to be incontrovertible."

Holmes smiled and patted my shoulder.

"My blushes, Watson. Nevertheless, I have given my word not to air his findings until the time is ripe."

This was not to be borne; I so far forgot myself as to clutch at the lapels of Holmes' dressing gown as I expostulated, "Holmes, I *must* know! Does he then consider Lizzie to be the murderess?"

Holmes smiled enigmatically.

"I fear that although the jury found her not guilty, the stain upon her character is likely to remain. Time will tell."

And with that I had to be content.

ABOUT THE AUTHOR/ILLUSTRATOR

Dixie, originally from Washington State, moved to California when she got married, where she raised three daughters. After she retired, she moved back to the Pacific Northwest.

Her hobbies include: drawing, writing, painting, reading, and book-collecting, not to mention seeing how much trouble she can get her hapless crimefighting cartoon heroes, Dahler and Nicholls, into...